CHRISTMAS CAROLS

FOR VIOLIN DUET

Arranged by Michelle Hynson

ISBN 978-1-5400-9736-1

Visit Hal Leonard Online at
www.halleonard.com

Contact us:
Hal Leonard
7777 West Bluemound Road
Milwaukee, WI 53213
Email: info@halleonard.com

In Europe, contact:
Hal Leonard Europe Limited
42 Wigmore Street
Marylebone, London, W1U 2RN
Email: info@halleonardeurope.com

In Australia, contact:
Hal Leonard Australia Pty. Ltd.
4 Lentara Court
Cheltenham, Victoria, 3192 Australia
Email: info@halleonard.com.au

ANGELS WE HAVE HEARD ON HIGH

VIOLIN

Traditional French Carol
Translated by JAMES CHADWICK

AWAY IN A MANGER

VIOLIN

Words by JOHN T. McFARLAND (v.3)
Music by JAMES R. MURRAY

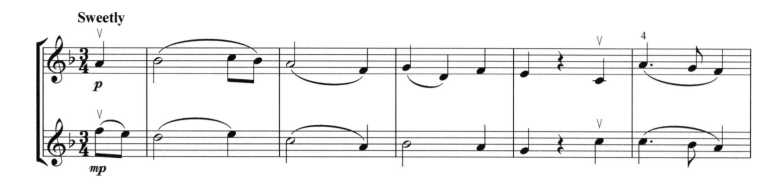

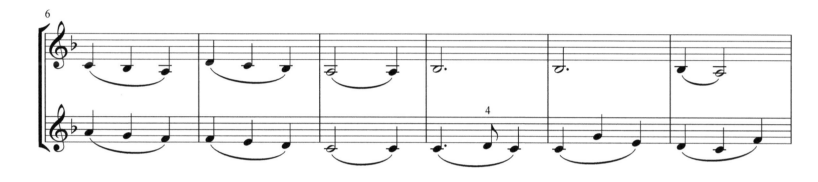

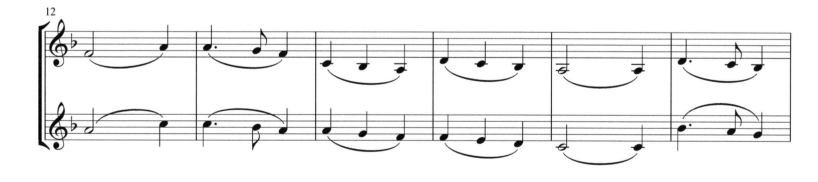

BRING A TORCH, JEANNETTE, ISABELLA

VIOLIN

17th Century French Provençal Carol

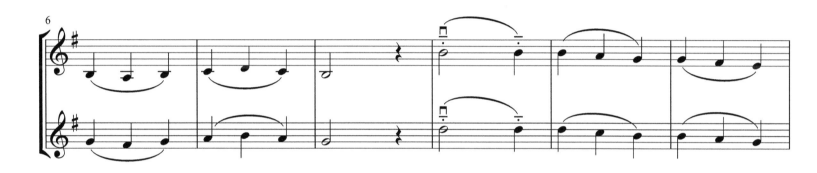

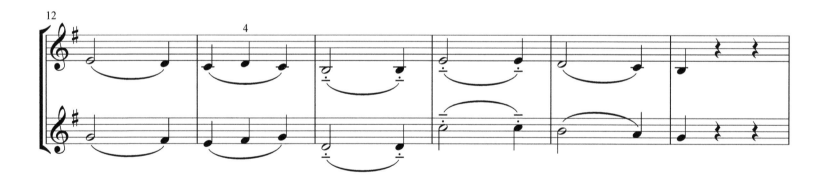

COVENTRY CAROL

VIOLIN

Words by ROBERT CROO
Traditional English Melody

DECK THE HALL

VIOLIN

Traditional Welsh Carol

DING DONG! MERRILY ON HIGH!

VIOLIN

French Carol

THE FIRST NOEL

VIOLIN

17th Century English Carol
Music from W. Sandys' *Christmas Carols*

Moderately slow

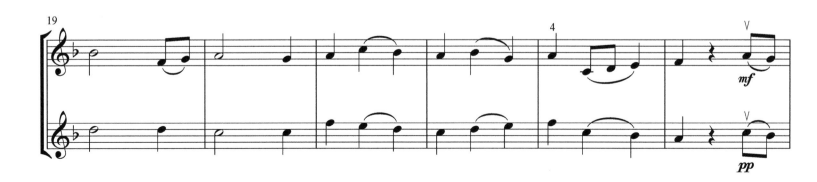

THE FRIENDLY BEASTS

VIOLIN

Traditional English Carol

GO, TELL IT ON THE MOUNTAIN

VIOLIN

African-American Spiritual
Verses by JOHN W. WORK, JR.

GOD REST YE MERRY, GENTLEMEN

VIOLIN

Traditional English Carol

GOOD KING WENCESLAS

VIOLIN

Words by JOHN M. NEALE
Music from *Piae Cantiones*

HARK! THE HERALD ANGELS SING

VIOLIN

Words by CHARLES WESLEY
Altered by GEORGE WHITEFIELD
Music by FELIX MENDELSSOHN-BARTHOLDY
Arranged by WILLIAM H. CUMMINGS

THE HOLLY AND THE IVY

VIOLIN

18th Century English Carol

I HEARD THE BELLS ON CHRISTMAS DAY

VIOLIN

Words by HENRY WADSWORTH LONGFELLOW
Music by JOHN BAPTISTE CALKIN

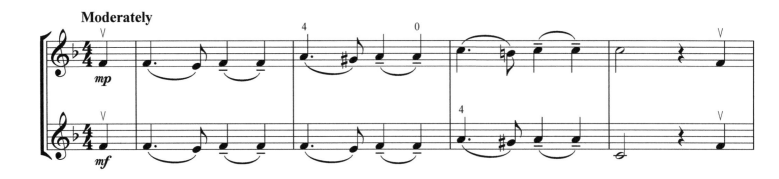

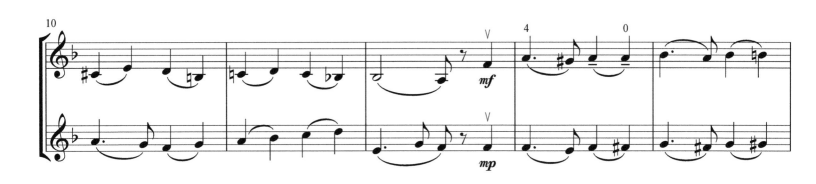

I SAW THREE SHIPS

VIOLIN

Traditional English Carol

IT CAME UPON THE MIDNIGHT CLEAR

VIOLIN

Words by EDMUND HAMILTON SEARS
Music by RICHARD STORRS WILLIS

JINGLE BELLS

VIOLIN

Words and Music by
J. PIERPONT

JOY TO THE WORLD

VIOLIN

Words by ISAAC WATTS
Music by GEORGE FRIDERIC HANDEL
Adapted by LOWELL MASON

O CHRISTMAS TREE

VIOLIN

Traditional German Carol

O COME, ALL YE FAITHFUL

VIOLIN

Music by JOHN FRANCIS WADE
Latin Words translated by FREDERICK OAKELEY

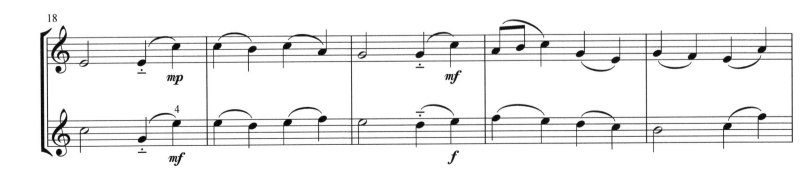

O HOLY NIGHT

VIOLIN

French Words by PLACIDE CAPPEAU
English Words by JOHN S. DWIGHT
Music by ADOLPHE ADAM

O LITTLE TOWN OF BETHLEHEM

VIOLIN

Words by PHILLIPS BROOKS
Music by LEWIS H. REDNER

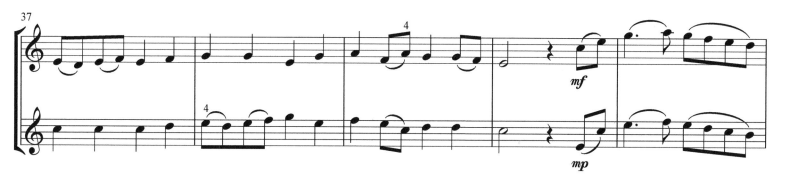

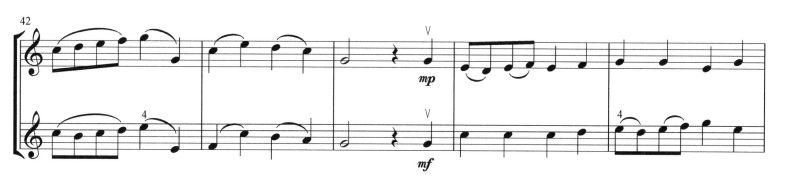

SILENT NIGHT

VIOLIN

Words by JOSEPH MOHR
Translated by JOHN F. YOUNG
Music by FRANZ X. GRUBER

SING WE NOW OF CHRISTMAS

VIOLIN

Traditional French Carol

STILL, STILL, STILL

VIOLIN

Salzburg Melody, c.1819
Traditional Austrian Text

UP ON THE HOUSETOP

VIOLIN

Words and Music by
B.R. HANBY

WE THREE KINGS OF ORIENT ARE

VIOLIN

Words and Music by
JOHN H. HOPKINS, JR.

WE WISH YOU A MERRY CHRISTMAS

VIOLIN

Traditional English Folksong

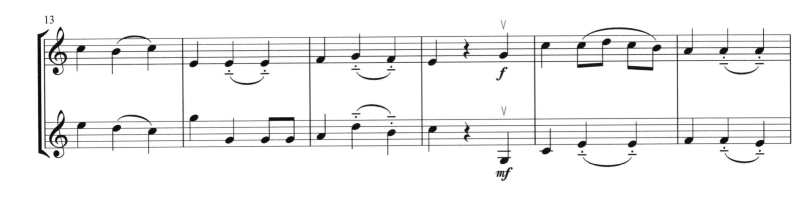

WHAT CHILD IS THIS?

VIOLIN

Words by WILLIAM C. DIX
16th Century English Melody

WHILE SHEPHERDS WATCHED THEIR FLOCKS

VIOLIN

Words by NAHUM TATE
Music by GEORGE FRIDERIC HANDEL

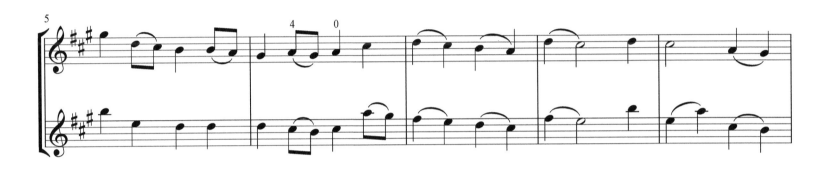

VIOLIN DUET

COLLECTIONS

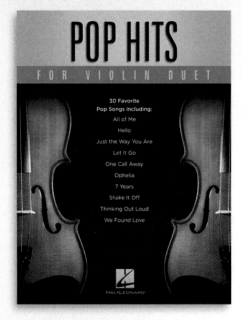

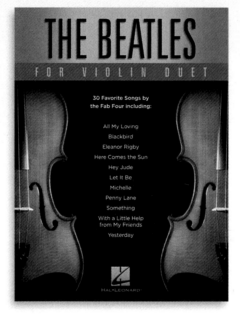

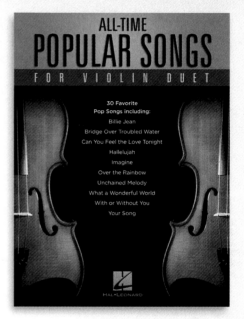

These collections are designed for violinists familiar with first position and comfortable reading basic rhythms. Each two-page arrangement includes a violin 1 and violin 2 part, with each taking a turn at playing the melody for a fun and challenging ensemble experience.

ALL-TIME POPULAR SONGS FOR VIOLIN DUET

Billie Jean • Bridge over Troubled Water • Can You Feel the Love Tonight • Hallelujah • Imagine • Over the Rainbow • Unchained Melody • What a Wonderful World • With or Without You • Your Song and more.

00222449 . . . . $12.99

THE BEATLES FOR VIOLIN DUET

All My Loving • Blackbird • Eleanor Rigby • A Hard Day's Night • Hey Jude • Let It Be • Michelle • Ob-La-Di, Ob-La-Da • Something • When I'm Sixty-Four • Yesterday and more.

00218245 . . . . $12.99

POP HITS FOR VIOLIN DUET

All of Me • Hello • Just the Way You Are • Let It Go • Love Yourself • Ophelia • Riptide • Say Something • Shake It Off • Story of My Life • Take Me to Church • Thinking Out Loud • Wake Me Up! and more.

00217577 . . . . $12.99

DISNEY SONGS FOR VIOLIN DUET

Beauty and the Beast • Can You Feel the Love Tonight • Colors of the Wind • Do You Want to Build a Snowman? • Hakuna Matata • How Far I'll Go • I'm Wishing • Let It Go • Some Day My Prince Will Come • A Spoonful of Sugar • Under the Sea • When She Loved Me • A Whole New World and more.

00217578 . . . . $12.99

www.halleonard.com

Prices, contents, and availability subject to change without notice.